HOTS

a ballad by
FLEUR ADCOCK
for music by
GILLIAN WHITEHEAD
with monoprints by
GRETCHEN ALBRECHT

BLOODAXE BOOKS

ISBN: 1 85224 001 6 *Hotspur*
       1 85224 000 8 *4-Pack #1*

First published 1986 by
Bloodaxe Books Ltd,
P.O. Box 1SN,
Newcastle upon Tyne NE99 1SN.

Bloodaxe Books Ltd acknowledges
the financial assistance of Northern Arts.

Hotspur was written for music by Gillian Whitehead,
and commissioned by Musicon with funds from Northern Arts.
It was first performed in Durham on 2 February 1981 by Gemini,
conducted by Peter Wiegold, with Margaret Field mezzo-soprano.
Sets using Gretchen Albrecht's monoprints were commissioned
by the New Zealand High Commission.

Typesetting by Bryan Williamson, Swinton, Berwickshire.

Printed in Great Britain by
Tyneside Free Press Workshop Ltd, Newcastle upon Tyne.

I

There is no safety
there is no shelter
the dark dream
will drag us under.

I married a man of metal and fire,
quick as a cat, and wild:
Harry Percy the Hotspur,
the Earl of Northumberland's child.

He rode to battle at fourteen years.
He won his prickly name.
His talking is a halting spate,
his temper a trembling flame.

He has three castles to his use,
north of the Roman Wall:
Alnwick, Berwick, Warkworth –
and bowers for me in them all.

I may dance and carol and sing;
I may go sweetly dressed
in silks that suit the lady I am;
I may lie on his breast;

and peace may perch like a hawk on my wrist
but can never come tame to hand,
wed as I am to a warrior
in a wild warring land.

High is his prowess
in works of chivalry,
noble his largesse,
franchyse and courtesy.

All this wilderness
owes him loyalty;
and deathly rashness
bears him company.

II

The Earl of Douglas clattered south
with Scottish lords and men at arms.
He smudged our tall Northumberland skies
black with the smoke of burning farms.

My Hotspur hurried to halt his course;
Newcastle was their meeting-place.
Douglas camped on the Castle Leazes;
they met in combat, face to face.

It was as fair as any fight,
but Douglas drew the lucky chance:
he hurled my husband from his saddle,
stunned on the earth, and snatched his lance.

I weep to think what Harry saw
as soon as he had strength to stand:
the silken pennon of the Percies
flaunted in a foreign hand.

'Sir, I shall bear this token off
and set it high on my castle gate.'
'Sir, you shall not pass the bounds
of the county till you meet your fate.'

The city held against the siege;
the Scots were tired and forced to turn.
They tramped away with all their gear
to wait my lord at Otterburn.

III

I sit with my ladies in the turret-room
late in the day, and watch them sewing.
Their fingers flicker over the linen;
mine lie idle with remembering.

Last night the moon travelled through cloud
growing and shrinking minute by minute,
one day from fullness, a pewter cup
of white milk with white froth on it.

These August days are long to pass.
I have watched the berries on the rowan
creeping from green towards vermilion,
slow as my own body to ripen.

I was eight years old when we married,
a child-bride for a boy warrior.
Eight more years dragged past before
they thought me fit for the bridal chamber.

Now I am a woman, and proved to be so:
I carry the tender crop of our future;
while he pursues what he cannot leave,
drawn to danger by his lion's nature.

Daylight fades in the turret-slit;
my ladies lay aside their needles.
They murmur and yawn and fold away
the fine-worked linen to dress a cradle.

And I should rest before the harvest moon
rises to dazzle me. But now
I stitch and cannot think of sleep.
What should I be sewing for tomorrow?

IV

It fell about the Lammastide –
the people put it in a song –
the famous fray at Otterburn,
fought by moonlight, hard and long.

The Percies wore the silver crescent;
the moon was a full moon overhead.
Harry and his brother were taken,
but first they'd left the Douglas dead.

Who was the victor on that field
the Scots and the English won't agree;
but which force won as songs will tell it
matters little that I can see:

it surges on from year to year,
one more battle and still one more:
one in defence, one in aggression,
another to balance out the score.

Crows flap
fretting for blood.
The field of battle
is a ravening flood.

There is no safety
there is no shelter
the fell tide
will suck him under.

V

He did not fall at Otterburn;
he did not fall at Humbledowne;
he fell on the field at Shrewsbury,
a rebel against the crown.

He might have been a king himself;
he put one king upon the throne,
then turned against him, and sought to make
a king of my brother's son.

Families undo families;
kings go up and kings go down.
My man fell; but they propped him up
dead in Shrewsbury Town.

They tied his corpse in the marketplace,
jammed for their jeers between two stones;
then hacked him apart: a heavy price
he paid for juggling with thrones.

Four fair cities received his limbs,
far apart as the four winds are,
and his head stared north from the walls of York
fixed on Micklegate Bar.

Now let forgetfulness wash over
his bones and the land's bones,
the long snaky spine of the wall,
earthworks and standing stones,
rock and castle and tower and all.

There is no safety
there is no shelter
the fell flood
has drawn him under.

Notes

Henry Percy, known as Hotspur, eldest son of the first Earl of Northumberland, was born on 20 May 1364. The Percies were of Norman descent; they controlled the north of England with something like kingly power for several centuries, first as feudal lords and then as Barons of Alnwick and later Earls of Northumberland. They have been described as 'the hereditary guardians of the north and the scourge of Scotland'.

Accounts of Hotspur's life appear in the *Dictionary of National Biography* and the *Complete Peerage* and, in a fictionalised form, in Shakespeare's *Richard II* and *Henry IV, Part I*. He was a valiant and precocious warrior, and soon became a favourite with the people. He held such positions as were consistent with his rank and descent – Governor of Berwick and Warden of the Marches – but his chief pleasures were warfare (against the Scots or the French or anyone else) and, as an incidental sideline to this, political intrigue. It proved his undoing. He was killed at the Battle of Shrewsbury on 12 July 1403 in an unsuccessful rebellion against Henry IV, whom he had conspired to put on the throne.

His character was not entirely admirable, to modern eyes: he had a tendency to change sides and to choose his allies according to their usefulness, disregarding former loyalties; and he was as brutal as any of his opponents when he chose: his fate of being quartered after his death was one which he had himself ordered to be performed on a defeated enemy. However, his personal courage and his even then slightly anachronistic devotion to the ideals of chivalry made him a natural focus for the legends which have clung to his name.

The ballad is sung in the person of his wife Elizabeth Mortimer (not Kate, as Shakespeare calls her). She was born at Usk on 12 February 1371 and was the daughter of the Earl of March and the granddaughter, through her mother, of Edward III. She married Hotspur in 1379 and they had a daughter (whose date of birth is not recorded) and a son, born in 1393 and named after his father.

I.

A halting spate: Hotspur was said to have some kind of impediment in his speech, which at times delayed his fiery utterances.

High is his prowess: This section quotes the traditional elements of the ideal of chivalry.

II.

Castle Leazes: The pasture-lands north of the city wall.

'Sir, I shall bear this token off...': The two speeches are taken from the version quoted by Froissart.

IV.

Otterburn: The battle was probably fought on the night of 19 August 1388, by moonlight.

Silver crescent: This was the cap-badge of the Percies; their coat of arms bore a blue lion rampant.

His brother: Ralph Percy.

V.

Humbledowne (or Humbleton, or Homildon Hill): The battle fought here on 13 September 1402 was Hotspur's revenge for Otterburn. The English won, capturing the 3rd Earl of Douglas (Archibald, successor to James, the 2nd Earl, who fell at Otterburn) and many other Scots.

He might have been a king himself: Not by legal succession; but if Elizabeth's nephew, the young Earl of March, had been set on the throne, Hotspur would very probably have been regent. In any case his popularity was such that the people could well have seen him as a possible king.

Four fair cities: After his body had been displayed in the marketplace at Shrewsbury it was buried; but a rumour arose that he was still alive, and his corpse was therefore disinterred and dismembered, and the four limbs sent to London, Bristol, Chester and Newcastle to be shown as evidence of his death.

Fleur Adcock was born in 1934 in Papakura, New Zealand. She grew up in New Zealand and England, and settled in London in 1963. In 1977-78 she took a year off from her job as a librarian at the Foreign Office to become writer in residence at Charlotte Mason College, Ambleside, in Cumbria, and in 1979 became a freelance writer. From 1979 to 1981 she lived in Newcastle, where she was the Northern Arts Literary Fellow and, when Gillian Whitehead held the Northern Arts composer fellowship, worked with her on *Hotspur*. They have since collaborated on operas and other musical works.

Her *Selected Poems* includes work from six previous collections, four published by Oxford University Press: *Tigers* (1967), *High Tide in the Garden* (1971), *The Scenic Route* (1974) and *The Inner Harbour* (1979). It also includes the Lake District poems of *Below Loughrigg* (1979).

The Virgin & the Nightingale, Fleur Adcock's verse translations of medieval Latin poets, appeared from Bloodaxe in 1983. Her latest collection is *The Incident Book* (OUP, 1986).

Gretchen Albrecht was born in 1943 in Auckland, New Zealand. In 1964 she graduated with a DFA Hons in Painting from the University of Auckland's School of Fine Arts, and was the School's Teaching Fellow in Painting in 1972-73. In 1981 she was the Frances Hodgkins Fellow at the University of Otago, Dunedin. She has shown paintings in numerous group and one-woman exhibitions since 1964 in New Zealand, Australia and America, and works as a full-time painter.

Ivy Leaves & Arrows

MAURA DOOLEY

BLOODAXE BOOKS

ISBN: 1 85224 002 4 *Ivy Leaves and Arrows*
      1 85224 000 8 *4-Pack #1*

First published 1986 by
Bloodaxe Books Ltd,
P.O. Box 1SN,
Newcastle upon Tyne NE99 1SN.

Bloodaxe Books Ltd acknowledges
the financial assistance of Northern Arts.

For Mary and Denis Dooley

ACKNOWLEDGEMENTS

Acknowledgements are due to the editors of the following publications in which
some of these poems have appeared: *Argo, Lancaster Literature Festival Anthology*
(1986), *Macmillan Junior Poetry Anthology for schools* vol. III, and *North*. 'The
Woman of Mumbles Head' won second prize in the 1986 Yorkshire Open
Poetry Competition

Typesetting by Bryan Williamson, Swinton, Berwickshire.

Printed in Great Britain by
Tyneside Free Press Workshop Ltd, Newcastle upon Tyne.

Cornwall. 1948

In Charlestown Bay the sea lapped in like milk,
Creamy with china clay. The beach a still small shell
At the end of a dusty street, curled up in the sun.

You crossed the country on your fiery Norton,
She was a crab on your back and her flowery dress flew,
All day long summer beat your hearts together.

And in the deepest bowl she cracked two eggs
First of the new days, fresh laid: war was over,
This sponge was lighter than any they had known.

In Truro shopkeepers shook out clean blinds like flags,
You chose ripe plums under their stripey shield and
Later buried the dull stones in warm sand.

But knowing they'd never grow green you climbed
To the tiny church's salty heights, your lips parched,
Your eyes aching, looking so hard for Lyonesse.

Changing Trains. April 1984

Over the bridge at Chepstow,
A marsh, a field, a bit of a wood,
And water spreading like a sheet:
Steel we've come from, steel we travel on,
Steel this is, you could walk on it.

'This knife wouldn't cut butter!'
My mother stabs at grey meat,
'When it runs,' my father, smiling,
Teases a curl from the yellow brick,
It clouds the shining chrome.

'I don't like that one,'
Its hard foot bit into his fist,
So bone-handled was the one he chose,
And creamy with age, soft on his tongue
For that forbidden lick.

At antique stalls, in junk shops,
I turn them over, Elkington, Tailor, Thompson,
Firth: fish knives are fish shaped
For paring and pulling,
Even glimpsed I smell Fridays.

Cathedral and glasshouse,
More grey, more green, then
Birmingham in bright blocks.
'Built on cars,' she says,
'And chocolate.'

But Mabel and Winnie
Have long since put their feet up,
Stopped bagging the Misshapes
In plain dark Bournville,
Factory in a garden.

MAURA DOOLEY

Your grandad helped design
A car that nestled on his leaving cake.
You keep the model still, on a shelf,
Dustless, but shift a Russian gear
To leave that town behind.

My Double Decker melts and
At Sheffield I change trains.
They said no to the miners
And their city glistens, a bowl of light,
The mouth of Hell's furnace.

Cold Meats

You, in the vinery, where I picture
The kitchen seedy but hear you talk
Pure, light, sharp as a knife.
You, lunching, a new Beaujolais
And napkins heavy with starch,
Slicing cold meats carefully.
You dancing, clear in a room
Livid with shadows, a bright
Blade through stale air.
You do it so well, you do it all,
While the Underground spreads
Like a tree through your veins,
But no leaf stirs.

Sugar Frosting

His small hard mouth
Is flushed with fruit,
His breath is sweet
With stolen strawberries,
He blows a dust of candy
On your neck, a sugar frosting,
And through it bites your flesh.
Down on the damp grass,
Through a tangle of leaves,
His hands stir and plunder.
The cheek you turn to him
Is downy with pale hair,
Stippled with freckles,
A Seurat of strawberry and rose.

Questions You Can't Answer

It used to be the highest mountain
Or the nearest planet. Holding the fruit
Between thumb and finger you told me
The earth is not round, the earth is not flat.
But why a blood orange? You sighed.
Laid your knife on a plate where crescents
Of peel were leaning, offering up their fat
Gondolas as your pared world.

                    And by now
I've learnt how to cut to the right depth,
How to prise my fingers between the segments
Which pull free, falling pale, diminished, pithy.
The thin skin of the fruit is streaked bloody
And, always clumsy, my hands run with juice.

Before me in the queue a nervous woman asks,
'Are those South African oranges?'
Smiling, he shakes his head.
'I know what you mean love, don't worry, we like
To know who's had their paws on them, don't we?'

Even That Routine

The roof is lipped with milk.
Never before such brightness,
So much of it, mulled here
By winter sun and hawthorn shadow
To the lightest cream.
Cooling, it forms a skin on my world,
Sits like a thatch on my slates,
Loops low over the bedroom window
A sail taut against the blue wind.

When you had wrung every drop from her,
Playing plain course gently, lightly,
I stood above the silvery pail
Milk lapping its sides,
Longing to plunge my arms
Into its feathery wet warmth.

Bored with even that routine
You sold her. Now the ice knits,
Now the snow thickens
Around her locked and silent shed.
It's cold and in the dusty pail
We carry in coal for our fire.

MAURA DOOLEY

Six Filled the Woodshed with Soft Cries

From grass-stained eggs we bred eight;
Two hens, six fine white cockerels,
They scrambled, fluffing feathers for
A summer and an autumn month.

Now, hands pinked by the wind,
I watch their maned necks nervously.
Yesterday the tiniest learnt to crow,
Latched a strange voice to crisp air,
His blood red comb fluting the wind,
Feathers creaming, frothing at his throat.

One month till Christmas, the clouds thicken,
He turns on me an icy, swivel eye,
Do you dare deny me?

My neighbour helps me chase them,
Snorting snuff, which rests on his sleeve
In a fine white scatter. A wicker basket
Gapes wide as he dives for them.
Six filled the woodshed with soft cries.
Their feathers cover stony ground
Like a lick of frost.

Ivy Leaves and Arrows

Fullest moon and winter snows
Feed the wind that nightly blows
Out the sun of steely will.

By first light, ivy leaves and arrows
Mark the strip of path that narrows
The sheets of field, billowing down the hill.

The wind has fallen, the air is still,
Only the cockerel shakes comb and quill,
Across the valley his morning music glows:

Warm on the knife-edge air it goes,
Vibrant with hunger and joy he crows
Over the field and trees so still,

And picks up lightly his crabby toes,
Printing with ivy leaves and arrows
The new-washed skirt of the hill.

MAURA DOOLEY

Early Morning

The garden rising from its bed of frost
Is green as a raw glass
Swilled with faint colour
And crude sparkle.
I run my eyes around its rim
And hear it ring.

Over the Fields

Whoever heard of a seamless garment?
This is a sky scabby with stars
And a moon that eats a hole in the grass,
A night announced by the drone of a plane
And lit by tail lights.
There's owl-screech and fox-bark,
Wake them and the geese will laugh
Blisters to your face. But the phone
Still rings, the television flickers,
And over the fields wires hum.

The Women of Mumbles Head

The moon is sixpence,
A pillar of salt or
A shoal of herring.
But on such a night,
Wild as the wet wind,
Larger than life,
She casts a long line
Over the slippery sea.
And the women of Mumbles Head
Are one, a long line,
Over the slippery sea.
Wet clothes clog them,
Heavy ropes tire them,
But the women of Mumbles Head
Are one, a long line,
Over the slippery sea.
And under white beams
Their strong arms glisten,
Like silver, like salt,
Like a shoal of herring,
Under the slippery sea.
And they haul
For their dear ones,
And they call
For their dear ones,
Casting a long line
Over the slippery sea.
But the mounting waves
Draw from them,
The mountain waves
Draw from them,
The bodies of their dear ones,
O, the bodies of their dear ones,
Drawn under the slippery sea.

MAURA DOOLEY

In a chain of shawls
They hook one in,
Fish-wet, moonlit,
They've plucked him back
From under the slippery sea.
For the moon is sixpence,
A pillar of salt or
A shoal of herring,
And the women of Mumbles Head
Are one, a long line
Over the slippery sea.

The women rescued a lifeboatman by making
a rope of their knotted shawls, after the
Mumbles lifeboat was lost in a storm in 1883

Fabricio Spinola flees from Ireland. 1588

A bank of licorice cloud threw wind and rain
And slammed the strand with waves all day. Tonight
High tide drew up a hundred crabs, a calf, a doll.

In such a storm the *Girona* settled down.
Gulls cast shrouds of mewing over the dead,
The broken boat oozed pearls among the rocks.

For weeks the sea breathed silver, gold and bone,
The flash of fins now dulled their eyes, they spread
Fine nets at the water's edge and prayed.

Spinola lay with his ship in his arms
And on islands of weed his ring floated in,
No tengo mas que dar te, I have nothing more to give thee.

But he left his mark in hair, eye, a salamander
Bloody with rubies, and gold, deep in the sand,
Where digging for lug we long for doubloons.

MAURA DOOLEY

A Boat to the Blaskets

His perfect English tells us he is Dutch,
And at his side the pale American
Reads of the Marabar caves while
Our little boat strokes a calm sea.
The quiet passage to a steep green island
Where we step through daisies, driving the sheep
Before us, to stand in the ruined houses,
And I want that face to be yours Peig.

Under the cliff we test the clear May water
With tiny cries, brave runs into the cold
Which carries a fulmar, a gannet, a gull.
With our eyes we comb the bay for seals or
Leave the hot white sand, picking like crabs
Along the crumbling path to find above the ruined houses
Two larks turning in the glassy air,
And I want to hear Tomás's foot on the soft grass.

The ferry is an hour late returning,
And we are beached on the slippery quay like shells,
Or strangers, glad of this clumsy company
As we stare at the ruined houses, silently.
We didn't see tall waves, a mad, black sea,
The mist that must have filled the stones like mortar,
Those broken nets. Only an empty picture frame,
A small carved bed, a hearth of cold ashes.

Kerry Blue

A slatey smoke-backed creature,
Lifting her delicate head
To the lavender sky. Under molten clouds
She is fading violets,
Or the dusty bloom on a damson.
Shaking her sea-coloured coat
Till it shines she might vanish
With the mist, leaving only her song,
A full green note on salt air.

St Brendan and the Angel

You cannot understand this bog
How it seeps under the rock and broods.
Or how this hand of stone simmers
In a cool sea, great slabs of it to tear
A leather boat or barb an angel,
Slapping at the waves, beaching the frail fish,
And the sun a crack in a stormy sky
Where Lucifer always falls, is falling now.

Vanished Lives

If we have no God, then we have ancestors.
She has lifted leather ledgers larger than herself,
Printed soft warm thumbs on each curled corner,
And back she goes through a century and half to 1837,
The last full stop.

        A roll of names that
Sent her to wet gravestones, her fingers feeling
For their vanished lives, but all is blurred here,
Made less distinct by granite, slate or mossy characters.
And the other side is darker still:

        Blight that rotted fields
And emptied cottages, the crowded quay, the salt-rinsed boat,
A letter home. No records kept in spiny copperplate,
No cross to show that's where they've been,
Only a face that's handed down and on,
Glimpsed in a glass dark: Brigid McTighe, her mark.

An Exile

Blaubeeren,
A bloom, a taste of sap rising,
Risen maybe, and wood and green shade.
We made syrup and jam
And it was like Alice's drink,
A sort of mixed flavour of cherry tart,
Custard, pineapple, hot buttered toast,
Everything nice you can possibly think of.

But best was that smoke sweetness,
Fresh from its light green bush
Rolled from cheek to cheek,
And our tongues long and blue.
In London we bought them in jars,
Polish, deep dark with promise,
And once, in such a smart shop,
I found them fresh and they cost –
Oh were so expensive and I carried
Them home, like glass, or a prize,
Their cardboard cradle blurred with juice,
I heaped white china bowls with them,
I relished the stains that bled on the cloth.
And so it was bitter to taste the dust,
The cool blandness of them,
And my heart wept.

Ah, but I ate each one slowly,
Stared deep in the mirror,
Oh, to step back I sighed, step through.
I looked hard at my tongue, long, tied, silent,
I looked hard at my tongue,
And saw it was blue.

Leaving Farmadine House

I woke to find this ship of a house sailing,
The red brick rich as a life's blood, glowing,
Sunlight making pearl of china,
Clinging to brass and to my hand on this
Delicate banister, spine of the house
That leads me down to morning.
My feet, a soft din on smooth wood,
Are the only words I can manage.

We breakfast with the green and gold,
Beads of warm milk lighten my coffee.
The sky is livery, heavy as my tongue,
The brick a sweeter red now and
I like the colours, I say. We stare at still trees,
Huge sycamore which hold attentive doves,
And on Jake's wire swallows gather.
We are all silent.

'You have to look at something
Until the shape of it is less ordinary,
Like repeating a word over to yourself
Until it becomes meaningless.'
Leaving, leaving, leaving, leaving.
Our own shadows are not ordinary.
Is there a stone that we cannot turn?
Perhaps this is the one, you say.

The quotation in the last stanza is taken from Gwen John's journal.

A Small Shaking of My Picture of the Kingdom

A small shaking of my picture of the kingdom;
Counters jarred a little, down a tiny snake
Or up a ladder. A straightening of spectacles,
A new page in the road atlas, women at a bus-stop,
More red brick or narrow lanes, a going-home of schools,
A blue or yellow bus, somewhere in England.
Against it all I shore what makes this home,
Wide light, a weaver's window, each stone in that wall.
This is the heart's small change,
A little silver saved against the rain.

Visiting

Watching the soapy swill trickle away,
Cloudy in soft water, a scum on hard,
Glittering over Armitage Shanks
Or Twyford's Vitreous Enamel.
And from the window a mountain,
A back wall, a square of blue sky somewhere,
Through net, through frosted glass,
Through an open window. Visiting.

Trying to imagine how it would be
To live out this life, I have
Loitered by estate agents' windows
And done up that old shack in spare weekends.
But in these distant friendly bathrooms,
Though I use your soap and borrow towels,
My toothbrush rests uneasy on the shelf.

Waiting

Inside we are burning the tree
That outside bends to hold safe
Its fruit in a raw summer,
And all the winds of Yorkshire
Shake a scent of applewood
About the damp house.

This wet July
I dare to place geraniums
Outside the swollen door.
Their petals scatter on my step,
You have to walk through flowers
To enter here.

It's other people's summer, not my own:
A wedding or move, a birth or job,
A teacup leafed with fears.
I work. I sleep. I cram more sheets
Into the Hotpoint's longing,
Straining to catch on the clammy air

Your knock at the door,
Your foot on the threshold,
Cradled in flowers.

Gypsophila Paniculata

What do they call this? Like ice or lace,
Its whitest petal is not as pale as you
Nor each thin stem as fragile. A florist's flower
It hangs from bridal hands, a summer dust.
But when you could no longer cloud a glass
They laid it round your tiny box like smoke,
And villagers' flowers, imperfect, bright,
Filled borrowed jugs and vases while
That frosted candy fizzed its saddest jest,
Gypsophila Paniculata, Baby's Breath.

MAURA DOOLEY

A Different Kind of Dark

We are strung out like leaves on a tree
Waiting for the sun to crisp them and
Knowing the time between to be a long decay,
One slip from green to gold and it's over.
Only the lazy man with the broom comes then,
Quietly he'll lock out the children and sweep up
The leaves, as the light thins, staggers, vanishes.
But a different kind of dark will follow,
Not this purple owl light with its fidgety moon,
And no treetops will hush them,
Nor nightingales lull them, only the wind
Will sometimes trouble them, rock or ruffle them,
Only the wind, Thomas, only the wind.

Second Generation

'There's just no fuchsia in it,' my Dad would joke,
But my dreams are hedged with red and purple,
Seal-lined, damp under blue mountains, caught like a burr
On this country's old coat that I try to shrug around me.

It's one long past of never having a future and
Taking the slow boat to a better land,
Needing to fill stomachs with something more than prayer,
Shedding a language, watching the shore grow small.

We want the tongue they took such care to lose,
To feel its shuffling sadness in our mouths,
We want to feel this greenness like a skin,
To scratch it when it itches, watch it heal.

Wearing the Claddagh ring, hoping its two hands
Would hold, not tear, this tiny heart,
Could I slip in there to watch the sea shift
Or cut some warmth out of a peaty soil?

No Siege of Ennis in the Irish Club,
No convent childhood, shamrock through the post,
Can net us back across that narrow passage
Nor make this town a place we can call home.

MAURA DOOLEY

THE LONG INTERVAL

S.J. Litherland

BLOODAXE BOOKS

ISBN: 1 85224 003 2 *The Long Interval*
        1 85224 000 8 *4-Pack # 1*

First published 1986 by
Bloodaxe Books Ltd,
P.O. Box 1SN,
Newcastle upon Tyne NE99 1SN.

Bloodaxe Books Ltd acknowledges
the financial assistance of Northern Arts.

For Dave Bell

ACKNOWLEDGEMENTS

Acknowledgements are due to the editors of the following publications in which
some of these poems have appeared: *Iron*, *Iron Anthology*, *Pitts*, *Poetry North-East*,
Reflections 2 and *Skylark*.

Typesetting by Bryan Williamson, Swinton, Berwickshire.

Printed in Great Britain by
Tyneside Free Press Workshop Ltd, Newcastle upon Tyne.

The Long Interval

The sea black and grey
in the spring night.
We watch the unformed
wave run feverishly.

Suddenly in the darkness
a mouth of light opens
and swallows itself
not wide enough to call.

We hear the faint smack
of its lips as the sound
is eclipsed by the dark
waters' rise and fall.

The sea black and grey
in the spring night.
In the darkness we wait
for a new mouth to alight

somewhere on the water
before drowning itself.
The vanished voice is heard
in the long interval.

The Trees' Small Cries

I wonder if I am pausing in winter
like a tree pauses, or rather is held
helpless by the air's betrayal.
Leafless arms seem in the glacier wind
to be small cries, solid as my breath.

Winter Walk

The cold wind, rough as glass-paper,
has scratched the sky,
and is a man's chin on my face.
The street is white and grey; its snow
run through by vehicles, frowns.
The townscape, in lines smudged by
darkness, stands rigid.
Even the snow creaks, at every step
like a staircase at night.

Autumn

It is Autumn and the
leaves snow down from the trees.
Once they burned with sadness
before winter. Yellow-headed
they were stripped slowly
and humiliated.

Control

The oblique to the perpendicular.
My heart swaying, held.

Elegy for Madroño

Summer home adieu.

My children, new-born, were baptised
in your sea. My despair was buoyant there.
Music rippled through the rooms brimming
to lift me to joy or to drown me.
In a picture on the wall I saw myself
helplessly pinned in the abstract cross
of a sailing boat, where the diagonal
of my sad passion swayed around my family.

In the sea my sorrow was soothed;
calm as my mother's motionless gaze
from the terrace, like a wind of tension
dropped, leaving the surface unbroken.
Only light shattered on the smooth,
gently vibrating water, striking a
flarepath for the morning sun. Swimming,
I doused the tiny lights in my body's
wave. Clear, ever-changing water would
chink at my side like money in a pocket.

Night time would persuade a chorus line
of fishing boats to emerge on the sea,
as if a magician coaxed a string of
lights to venture on his dark stage.
Later, we would play Beethoven
as a tribute to the moon, white as
a clown, casting relief on a warm night.
Moonlight a pearl shade for the eyes
to see gently what was unbearable by day.

Tension of meeting storms ahead and behind.
My father, the receding conflict, threats
growing ever fainter echoed in departing

thunder, while clouds massed on my marriage
skyline. There was no escape from the August
harvest of summer warmth meeting head-on
the cold inward summit of winter.
Our sleep was wrecked by lightning
thick as a man's wrist, plunging
into water with poker heat.

My son's joy was for tea in the early
hours while the storm flickered its
Broadway lights. Promise to wake me
was his cry, when the great thunder heads
grouped like wrestlers at the edge of the
sky. Rain oceans would flood past our
shutters, drowning windows in green light
like exit signs in a darkened cinema.
Excitement in every ghostly face as the
heavens shuddered for our entertainment.

Spain changing over the years, from
the closed, poor society; cart tracks,
fiestas, fascists thick as the flies,
shaded bars, empty countryside and beaches,
to the makeshift urban sprawl leaving its
tidemark on the coast; new spenders,
tables in the sun, and late democracy come
overnight with freshly erected red flags
in the square, tarmac shimmering like oil
on the sea. Two-sided change spent freely.

Tourists are the new Vikings, staying
for a fortnight to pillage the land,
the shanty towns at summer's end
are closed and exhausted; a dust
bowl creeps across the valley, once
farmed, claiming countryside and cottages,
once homes. Hotels have choked the old
life. Some, themselves, die of thirst,
raddled, unfinished skeletons stand
at crossroads warning the intruder.

My mother, distant observer, whose inner
turmoil never broke surface, calm face
turned to calamity, played music to drown
voices. She closed curtains to shade the sky,
closed windows and doors despite the heat,
endured the stifling air in preference
to the breeze which lifts the veil; mourning
her dead friends with stoicism which shuts out
the bright world. Reverence, only reverence,
secretly paid in a great debt, and overpaid,
to embalm griefs too mighty to decay.

Her eyes would watch her daughter and sigh.
I, useless sufferer, would retch troubles
like a permanent invalid. Why not try
sun-bathing, try swimming, try drink?
A mother taxed to minister to her ailing
child like a plant wilting in either
sun or shade, despite care, despite water,
refusing to stand upright, despite youth
and the season. She with her gardening
prowess, baffled by unreasonable distress.

Antonia, our Spanish friend, with old values,
and her father, Don Miguel, old autocrat
with dignified kindness who rides a new
motorbike. He rules from afar the village
cafés where we cannot pay for a single drink.
He spoils the children with ice-cream cake
and *leche fria*. At home his table is crowded
with *fiestas*. The old ways still dominate,
after food and wine the guitars are taken ˙
down, old choruses remembered and Antonia
steps out a childhood dance now folklore.

Antonia, green-yellow eyes fierce as a cat
when provoked; her anger sharp as their claws
also shows wounds. She protects her hunger
for love. Unmarried, she is still sworn
to her fiancé drowned in the Civil War. Her
loyalties clash with ours. Two-sided change

brings release from village purdah, new friends,
haute couture and cash. But she mourns the lost
customs, which like the olive trees with their
ancient roots, were proven and productive.

From the house an orchard falls to the pines
still tended above the shore's hotel mark.
An avenue leads to *Es Carregador*, the beach
too humble for development, protected by the
skirts of local cottages owned by grandmothers
unwilling to move. They rock on their patios,
call on the evening air like harsh crows
while the sea rustles at their feet, crimping
its wave to touch the same rock as the beach
sidles underneath. Seaweed ribbons deck the
gritty sand where an elderly tree overhangs.
Few tourists here, too far from the promenade.

The sea glitters in the bay, needle-sharp,
patches of Oxford and Cambridge blues
over rock and sand. In the water glass-green,
clear to the bottom, despite the yearly
encroachment of rubbish, flung up in a storm
like a council tip, mainly black oil and plastic.
Once, we struggled to launch an old wooden boat,
heavy as iron, and broke the gap-toothed winch;
old ways forgotten. Next year fibre-glass took
Antonia to sea to give her bottles decent burial.

Daughter possessed to draw when the music
drowns the room in its sparkling waves.
She, feverish with her pencil, draws
the sprites of love which sing, unknown
to her, for my ears alone the brimming
joy which killed the sailors and is now
calling me. I am in a whirlpool, watching
as my friends see me drown, through my
globe of swirling water I see their
alarmed faces, my mother's puzzlement.

We labour on the hillside behind Madroño.
Last year's path cut again by green thorns.
The sun making us slaves at noon. Forced
to pause we notice the sea has crept behind
us over the sky. Husband and I lift rocks
to line the path half-way completed.
Our plan is to reach the summit one year
to build a camp. The thorns return in winter
rain and clasp over the path. Now the hillside
remains locked where our labours are buried.

The evening of arrival scented by close pines;
gentle patio lamps throwing halos of soft
light onto shining tiles. The pure air flows
through the newly opened windows. Outside, warmth
and darkness tenderly wrap around the brilliant
plumage of the house. Pictures, cushions, glass
and cabinets gleam with colours like flowers.
In beautiful array, like sultans among gorgeous
tapestries, we drink tea and the fragrant air.

News from Mallorca is of further change.
This time tiny *Es Carregador* is threatened.
The sacred woodland paths will be cleared,
the land urbanised up to the rocky headland
we call the mountains of the moon. Once
so remote, its bouldered valley, discovered
only by those seeking barrenness where
thoughts remain unexpressed, will be
overlooked by tall arc lamps, mechanical
intruders from the town, heralding grid
plan streets and a camp of bungalows.

Who will save it while it still lives?
Before the last gasp is throttled from
the land by concrete, until it lies
like mortar itself, unyielding to the eye.
We see beauty beaten into a desert to
our senses, so that we are dying for
the long lost contour, buried by man

with the instinct of a parasite destroying
its host, dying without the wilderness
our strength has not yet deflowered.

Antonia, we talk of *Soller*, my first love
of the island and jealously you say: do not
forget *Capdepera*. Do you think three months
of young delight with mountains, hot sun and
heady blossom will sway a matron whose children
have grown here while her body becomes solid
with experience? If I remember the slender
affair of *Soller*, will I forget the long years
of marriage to *Capdepera*?

Madroño; old ghost, now shuttered
with a few dried plants, paintwork
peeling like sunburn, forlorn under
the towering pines. Lost love, a
familiar bend in your drive stops
the heart more than the death-closed
frontage and the back looking like
an empty shop after liquidation.

We return, Madroño, and life has moved
on without you. Antonia, more gaunt,
in lively argument against the new
socialist mayor. As she brings the
breakfast of *ensaimadas*, the new
street names are denounced, the Spanish
replaced by native *mallorquin*
which explodes in several contractions:
such as *Es Pla' D'en Coset* and
for the first time renounces the
homely reign of her natural tongue.

[*Madroño, Capdepera, Mallorca.*]

La Farmacia

Cool as a vault in summer
always the same temperature
like the *Cuevas de Artá*,
or an English cathedral.

The centrepiece of the house,
the formal dining room,
polished and chill as glass,
stands on marble tiles.

Surrounded by small, never
entered rooms, shuttered
against the street and sun
become dormant over years.

The concrete courtyard grey
in shadow has only the late
evening sun, a stroke crosses
the table like a sundial hand.

Don Miguel sits with his paper
reading imperfectly the poor
print at his time of rest.
He rustles the pages at our

entrance, with the nervous
tremor of age and to find
the darkness holds a guest.

[*In memory of Don Miguel, La Farmacia, Capdepera.*]

S J LITHERLAND

Ghosts at La Esquina

Night vigil in the bare room,
under the stark blue "daylight"
bulb the room looks innocent
of shadow as a young face.

In one corner the white walls
are puffed and corroded, they
decay, untouched by ornament,
with old-maidish chastity.

Not asleep I enjoy the size
of a small girl in the double
bed where the only breath
reaching my ear is the sea.

Fifty years closed in a drawer
the virgin sheets are iron
mottled, their youth preserved
in her slender initials

stitched with a flourish at
each edge and the crochet trimmings
spraying over the bedspread,
wavelets from a spring long dead.

My earliest memory recalls
the whitewashed damp walls
of an air-raid shelter, smell
of iron corroding, cement floor

as here, with the light bulb
burning "like day", whispers
of subdued conversation
breaking near like the sea.

A comforting rise and fall
of murmuring voices settled
around the paraffin stove
after my father's urgent run

across the street, ferrying me
in his arms. The danger and he
have perished forty years on
but the tranquillity returns

unlocked like her preparation
for womanhood from its grave.
He was buried here, shut in
a hillside drawer, a cupboard

for Protestants in the Catholic
cemetery. His corner is softened
by an oleander tree and the slot
faced with marble and lettered.

Some are marked with only
a hasty scrawl of name and date,
blurring in concrete, as if
a clerk registered them in.

Who deserves such a fate?
La Esquina crumbles to slow
ruin and Antonia's childhood
memories are not passed on.

The tombs overlook the sea
under a hilltop of pine trees
scorched by a summer fire
into an arid autumnal frieze.

It is rumoured the fire leapt
from five points to devour
the green wood, some private
houses, and the village dead.

Their families fought all night
to save the hill from charring
its treasury of aisled shrines,
crosses, flowers and photographs.

In such flames Coventry once
harshly burned at the edge
of my childhood sky. We filed
silently from the shelter into

the gold glare of the melting
city's horizon. My father
lifted me onto his shoulder
and knew that I would remember.

Death at Mortlake

(for Michael Ford)

The river links past and present.
The tide is now poised at Mortlake,
the head of the water lowers
as it runs out of strength.

Two miles down river we lived,
twenty years downstream, not
dreaming of your future suspended
on the rising flood to Mortlake.

The river ascends stealthily,
we often watched the banks
crumble to its touch as midstream
the race was on to its source.

Flotsam journeying back and forth
would ride the brown, slippery
hide of the water, submerging
slowly as it drank and fell.

Above Mortlake, out of steam,
the current is reversed while
all the river awaits motionless
the decision to descend.

The pulse stops here of our past.
After a brief ceremony your
coffin glides out of reach,
beyond the press of a switch;

as you died, submerged beyond
a change of mind, you drifted
too long and could not reverse
the slow poison of your suicide.

You are carried with your few
flowers like a stick lifted
on the flood. Outside, as we
leave, the flowers reappear,

snatched from cremation, line
the path like small infants
schooled to hold up a message
beyond their comprehension.

Such a funeral-worn spot for
a ticket to state *In the memory*
of as if you signified
this little, passing, tribute.

I was afraid you would turn up,
miniaturised in an urn,
as if the ash of a person
were the essence, when the best

has already burned into memory,
and the rest to heat, smoke and
silky air. But your only flotsam
was the flowers. I took mine

to throw on the river's body
to catch the ebb and so return
each tide lower until buried.
The water had withdrawn from

the island, its slope of mud
and pebbles sweating a heavy
scent. Seagulls circled sensing
an event as I launched the small

packet in sight of our former
moorings. It clung to the shore,
eddied like an upturned paper
boat until I drove it with

a stone. I remember now, on
our wedding morning I found
a drowned man, driven in with
the debris, floating swollen

and red, become part of the
river's rough passage, delivered
here by the whim of the tide
where your unhappiness began.

January Snow

(for Frances Horovitz, 1938-1983)

Only cars destroy the snow
this Sunday, swishing a dark
track across the salted
street while walkers indent
a variety of marks.

What flight of thought lit
the cold bleak winter
with such delicate beauty,
transformed the steel
of rain into feathers?

At the moment the cold
would penetrate the heart
the blow softens and we
are showered with a vision
as if the trees of heaven

forfeited their blossom.
The ice of winter is not
cut and the sky will never
brighten today, but trees
display their ermine arms,

every bush carries a white
counterstroke to shadow
and every building blown
in the blizzard realigned
by a natural draughtsman.

It is the gentle material
of survival, fleece against
the arctic cold; perfectly
formed to astound the artist
in every person's soul.

We tread marks in new snow
as if breaking into silence
of a world beyond life,
human against inhuman form –
listening for the echo

that continues existence;
as I sat in my destroyed
car a year ago, unprepared
as the road for the snowfall
quietly laying sheets over

dead tracks, the windscreen
smashed like ice, splinters
clinging to my face, deaf
in the silence to the car
horn unstoppably crying

under my mouth until born
far-off as a headache.
I had imagined death but
life had blown onto my shut
eyes its fresh, chill draught.

Snow returns this January
a shock in the gloom
of flurries light as ash
to grace my anniversary
with wild confetti.

It survives its admirers
although cold bouquets melt
to the touch like a spirit,
falls outside my window
in heavy fabric of lace.

We vanish into silence
when death cancels shadow,
breaking the anguish
of our scars and wounds
to scatter us like snow.

Sea-Change

The thin waves glided over the flat sand,
finely overlapping, each layer of water
laid bare, so thin that glass was a frozen
parody of its silken translucence. Finer
than feeling this water was cut, laid on
the level beach indifferent to its beauty.

The waves flared from the shallow flow
where light twisted to a fine mesh,
tightening when the sea was hauled back.
Stranded in the sand were a few, flying
pebbles, their wings sunken as long trail
marks, preserved like pinned butterflies.

The Dream

I walked beyond the private theatre,
along an elegant, vaulted path
descending to a more private place
where you lived apart, standing serene
in a garden of stone. How graceful
was this walkway, a dream of modern
architecture elevated to beauty,
it was the sparest of poetry
taking flight, the purity of line
daring to curve towards delight.
You stood surprised, reserved,
in your garden, poised as a statue
among the abstract pattern of stones.
The beauty of form was revealed,
the balance of order performed.
You and I were reconciled.
We talked respectfully of private
lives, arranging our conversation
with delicacy like a Chinese game.
You are the poet at the centre
waking me to truth after a dream.

The Waterfall

The river in flood, stronger than agitation,
as if scorned, wrestles with humiliation,
out-pouring anger in relief, surges on,
does not pause, is the great cataract
of grievance, in its torrent grief.

We hear the waterfall above its roar,
a premonition of force catapulting
beyond wildness, beyond frenzy, out of sense,
a million thoughts shattered, self exploded
out of self, the moment split indefinitely.

Out of control the river rages over rocks,
littering its bed with snowdrops of spray
or calling up a race of spouts to its source;
higher, we see dark amber in its threshes
of foam, turning cream, all tumult,

pools pitching and steaming, in the crush
of water intricate ferns of cross currents
poised in the surf; the torrent cannot pause,
smashing from the overblown waterfall,
arching to the flow, which cannot fall,

compulsively seizes the force in blast
and freeze, and to the mind frees suddenly,
advances to the eye with its hair shook wild,
jumping the threshold of appearance,
dissolving distance and control.

Spring Force

Something in the air that burns, Spring
is more fierce here, the copper beech
is bright red, yet people walk beneath
unaware of an outrageous Impressionist
tree. Amid the day I see the night
of your eyes, a blackness of Spring
impossible to shield, unnerving fire.

The trees are choked with blossom,
I have never seen Spring gasp like this,
the tide so high; flowers bury leaves.
Yesterday the breeze caught the petals
in a snowstorm and in their showering
I see the autumn of the beech, refired,
and ash of the jet of your eyes.

The Vase

In a vase of arranged flowers
there is peace I cannot find;
even in your arms I imagine
an anxiety beyond calming.
What you call from me is riot;
an increasing burden of desire
growing wildly without sight.
Yet in your graceful limbs,
dark eyes, long tapering hands
fine as porcelain, you hold
this flowering of my senses,
a reawakening of the unquiet;
fearful joy living for a day.

JILL MAUGHAN

Ghosts at four o'clock

BLOODAXE BOOKS

ISBN: 1 85224 004 0 *Ghosts at four o'clock*
      1 85224 000 8 *4-Pack #1*

First published 1986 by
Bloodaxe Books Ltd,
P.O. Box 1SN,
Newcastle upon Tyne NE99 1SN.

Bloodaxe Books Ltd acknowledges
the financial assistance of Northern Arts.

'Hill End' won joint first prize in the 1984 Newcastle *Evening Chronicle*
Poetry Competition, and was first published in the *Evening Chronicle*.

Typesetting by Bryan Williamson, Swinton, Berwickshire.

Printed in Great Britain by
Tyneside Free Press Workshop Ltd, Newcastle upon Tyne.

To the memory of my father

Hill End

If our coming was a spring, then our going is well caught
in this biting season, though our small embrace
meets poorly with the features of this vast, moorland face,
with its voice as penetrating as a raging, windy day,

and its hill top snow like the white hair on a wise man's head.
But the stone wall lines that cut like secateurs
tell of a kind of inextractable pain, walking here with you,
crossing these icy patches, and even in our knowing

we have a hundred miles to go and a lifetime, none of this
compares to what is wrought in the iron stare of this place.
Our years are hardly a graze on this skin and our
energy almost a trespass on this living silence.

But our purpose as much as our past is breathing
on the haunting road of this familiar route,
and is breathing too, in the house at the end of the hill,
which is "sold" and to which we will not return.

Vase

Sometimes I think I will be here forever,
always like this, permanent and sure of tomorrow,
and the house too, unmovable and resilient.
The roses that flare up the stone walls
will return each summer, and sometimes
I can barely believe this will change.

But yesterday, having caught a glance
of someone else's despair,
I lay awake and fear blew in from
the open window, and I turned and tossed
but saw life sweep away in the shadows
that sailed across the stone walls,

and there I saw myself weak at the knees,
shorebound and alone, with many important words
left unsaid, and a mass of untied threads
clutched like promises,
and loves that wailed down the years,
all broken and fragmented pieces of a vase
I had once thought could not shatter.

Clocks

How many times have we looked at clocks?
Clocks on walls or waistcoats,
clocks hanging from chains
or staring from stretching steeples,
clocks that chime, buzz and toll.

And how they measure us, these infuriating
ticking mechanisms, we all revere
their authority; even the great, the powerful,
the perfect, have appointments to keep, one eye
always on the clock. We try

to keep them servile, wearing them
in spectacular gold or cool silver,
in computer faces we can press on
and off; we force them into fashion
and own them like pedigree dogs.

But behind the inoffensive ten to five
there's the curled lip and snarl
of places unvisited, dreams not captured,
moments that stabilised, but briefly, and passed,
and time running out.

Through this impartial lidless eye
the seconds are opening and closing,
at once propelled onwards, like
a fog's mantle shutting as you pass,
leaning forward before you.

And what an unstoppable force time is,
like an inexhaustible Arabian horse
with the silvered bit between its teeth,
clattering by on legs like pistons,
perfect stride after stride.

And all our clocks ticking in grinning harmony,
clocks that can wail or sing
make people come and go, suns rise and sink,
clocks that turn seasons inside out,
upside down. Clocks!

Two doors up

She hasn't been free from these walled
boundaries of home for seven years,
she talks to me through cold glass;
once she silently held up a photograph
of the man she had loved and lost.

Hers is a hollow life which harbours itself
in our short street,
passing the window you might glance in
to see her sitting over a low fire
wringing her knuckled anxious hands together,

or staring into flames that leap like
troubled memories from the hearth.
The television animates a world
which scares her and she says
she can't be bothered with the papers.

She is built like a thin winter bird,
white and grey and scared, she sits
in the house and waits for visitors
that don't come or is woken restlessly
by ghosts at four a.m.

In one man's view she is nothing
but a fool for not getting out or throwing
aside despair like a jacket
and perhaps in his hard, cold truth
he is right,

or then perhaps one day his world will
crumble too, and finding himself
weeping into a starched pillow
he will come to understand the old woman
two doors up, who never went out.

JILL MAUGHAN

Passing the house

The house has a voice, a silver tongue
that welcomes and says farewells,
an eye and a character.

It is built with bricks which have swallowed
whole voices, laughter and sorrows
and held them ever fast like a diary.

But nothing is legible, no tell-tale gossip
escapes from this throat, silence
is promised and kept.

Inbetween these walls, in the cement
that fills the cracks, there are
secret tears and passions that fell foul,

and growing up years, untidy as adolescence,
have scratched themselves into the building,
vague etchings on an earth's thick skin.

In our garden the 'perpetual strawberries'
flower like a legacy, the walls are haunted
with our tiny ineffectual promises,

late nights, the dying embers, bad wine
and conversations that we thought
rambled like walkers off the map.

Now swept along on a fast road
I glance quickly back at the house
and know part of us is embraced there,

that despite our going some truth stays behind,
stokes up the fire and breathes steadily
across the long fallow fields.

Ghost of love

Go home, ghost of love and sleep,
sleep for a lifetime and more
for we are finished and done.

The next time you come
floating in from nowhere,
I will snap my fingered thoughts

and drive you out,
I'll turn away and away
and if you dance around me

like a moth in the light
I will aim my strength
at your heart

and drive this stake
right through that part
of our love that still ticks on.

So go home, ghost of love and sleep,
sleep for a lifetime and more
for we are finished and done.

If you come trackless
through the forests
or snaking your way under my door,

if I wake beside you
one more morning,
I'll stab us open to the core

and then you will weep
my shade of love
then you'll weep

follow the winds or
climb a sunshaft to the sky
but turn your shadowy back on me,

and go home, ghost of love and sleep,
sleep for a lifetime and more
for we are finished and done.

JILL MAUGHAN

Gold

It is November but still the sun pours down
and the sky parades rebel blue
against the falling leaves and the dying season.
Only the dogs and the beck move
animated amongst the stillness,
you and I lean on the ancient bridge
and let time flow by.

We have given ambition its head, and success
sparkles on the edge of the day,
our separate roads constantly nag
to be travelled and chances haggle to be
realised. The past that brought us here
and the future that will drive us away

are hailed down for a moment:
as our shadows stretch across the grass
and the years turn to seconds
it is this brief starting-gun thrill
which holds us like a photograph;
when the shutter snaps closed
we shall be gone forever, chasing gold.

All roads

All roads lead to you,
even the ones to the sky,
even the ones that try
to climb mountains,
even they lead to you.

All the roads that wind
or crawl or charge
across this planet
bring me back to you.

I try them all,
the foreign ones,
the sure-as-hell ones
but they come back to you,
they come back to you.

JILL MAUGHAN

On your birthday

On your birthday I drank champagne
with him and laughed
until the tears dripped,

I walked through meadows
ripe as fruit, dashed
irritating flies aside

lay in the high grass
and watched foals flicking
their silly tails.

I sobered slowly, talked
too wildly, ran back
the years like a video,

saw myself on screen
and you too –
I was walking home

through the barley fields,
we had a 'home', it sat
like a vase on a table

and flowers bloomed from it,
the air was sticky
with close heat, but the house

was as cool as water
and you lived there.
On your birthday I never

drank to you, or sent you
a card or gave myself up
to more than

the thinnest regret,
but I remembered,
I remembered all the same.

Letters

The old letters are crumpled paper relics,
cast-offs and orphans,
they are cats' eyes in the darkness,
winking out of the backlog years
drawing me through all their endless corridors.

They pout in their bitter sweetness,
contest the present with their certain charms
and even if wooed from every side
they would still have me, these haunting
ex-loves, these childhood friends.

Don't look back, chatters life, *don't look back*,
so I read them guiltily and grow sad
wondering *whatever happened to* . . .
and fold them away with an affection
that is quickly wiped aside

as it grows plain it is safer to look ahead
than back, one day perhaps years on
the old letters will call to me
from their dusty house and I will go
to that place where time contorts in their grasp.

JILL MAUGHAN

A small death

The cat which no one's bothered to bury
has rotted unceremoniously
at the side of the field.

Each morning we've passed it's faded
a little, become more pained as if
tired by its struggle to remain.

At first we had curiosity, we noticed its patchy
colourings, the way it could have been
anyone's homely pet.

Even its fall into death didn't look
too startling, more as if it were
nudged rudely or jarred into perpetual sleep.

But lately that's all changed, now its fur
has rotted to transparent thin leather
and its mouth stays frozen in a long

lipless scream, its teeth are broken white bars
where the flies enter and the air that chances
to breathe over it is rapidly hurt.

Now our curiosity has fled. We stare
into the morning sun, walk wide
of the rancid air, we try to leave this small death

well alone, but it follows us along our path
and lingers in the corner of our eyes,
like a small stain on white, it stays.

Old feelings

Then old feelings are echoes,
caught as if in a sea-shell
or a beach cave, where the real voice
shouted, returns estranged.

Echoes which are shy to float back
into the conscious harbour,
like a boat its sails blowing in
the resistance of a hostile wind.

The angry odds toss it this way and that,
and its fragile frame rocks
on the waves and the wail of the weather,
now fierce and cold and unwelcoming.

And I am apart, watching distanced,
poised to turn away and never care
if it founders and fails, if it dies
or sinks without leaving its trace,

for I won't sail in it again
nor be a part of it, nor ever wholly
trust to its memory but still I hesitate
and stare, and seem to care

beyond all measure that what's there
remains. I want to warn it,
to turn it from these charged waters,
to send it back, saved.

JILL MAUGHAN

Death of a neighbour

When death calls in the four a.m. dawn
and you have expected him,
waited to feel his cold hand

on your shoulder,
then you leave
and in leaving

tread through the locked doors
and across the lawn,
hesitate by the garden chairs

and turn, to look
at the house in the June air,
only the horses see you go

as they snort and stare;
inside the tears and anguish of loss
are spilling, the ambulance

lights glare across
the lawn, but still
no one sees you departing.

Fly

I have nothing to say, I am a mute
travelling light and not
very far up in the world's atmosphere.

If you look to me for an explanation
I can give no satisfaction,
for I am just here

climbing up this see-through wall,
expecting no clearing to open,
no death to come easy,

expecting nothing from you.
Analyse, philosophise,
categorise me,

but you won't come any closer
to knowing me, and when you're done
be done with me without a qualm,

for I am not an endangered species,
there are millions of me,
we make our small entrances and exits

without celebration, and if
you destroy me in a shrug
of annoyance don't fret

for I will be back,
I'll come flying in one humid day
buzzing stupidly, buzzing,

buzzing like a foolish man
convicting himself, and if you kill me
again, then I'll come back again, again.

The horses

I have gathered a stable of unspoken sentences
which like unbroken colts
career in seasonless meadows
and paw uneasily at an impervious skin.

And how sorry I am that I never bridled
them better than this, gained something
of their trust and backed them well enough
to ride them into argument,
or submit them like an apology.

For they are to be sure, the best horses,
their blood more pure and passionate
in their veins, their spirits indomitable, so
we could have gone like truth into an attractive lie.

But these are the horses it takes courage
to mount, for there is huge risk
in these untamed
snorting, snatching stallions,
so full, so full of power.

Out in the fog

Out in the fog I watch the sea
acting out his feral cat fantasy;
when children tease him with stones
he leaps to snatch them from the cliffs
baring a wave of white teeth,
his growling lips pushed back.

His mouth breathes fog
like cigarette smoke
and in the blind air
the long wail of the foghorn
calls and is answered,
is answered and calls,

but I go on along the cliff edge
flirting with these dangerous elements
that strive to break their harness:
the mist eats up my way, the sea
beats threat against my freedom,
they leave me out in the fog and partly afraid.

Up here there is neither safety nor danger
but some of both, up here
neither the firm glow
of a summer nor winter's full
aggression but some of both,

and later, heading home across
a thread of beach, the water
stretches to claim me
and falls back empty-handed and angered;
again and again he breaks forward
with the violent waves of his body.

He attacks without conscience,
but tomorrow he will be passive
and smiling again,
to all outward appearance
the perfect gentleman.

JILL MAUGHAN